GW00692193

TOUCHING ON LOVE

David Clarke

David Clarke

TOUCHING ON LOVE

David Clarke

HIPPOPOTAMUS PRESS

ACKNOWLEDGEMENTS are owed to the editors of the following magazines: *Acumen, Envoi, The Frogmore Papers, Iota, Links, Northern England 2000, Orbis, Other Poetry, Outposts Poetry Quarterly, Pennine Platform, Poetry Nottingham International, Seam, Smiths Knoll.*

First published in 2002 by
HIPPOPOTAMUS PRESS
22, Whitewell Road,
Frome, Somerset, BA11 4EL

ISBN 0 904179 67 2 Pbk
        0 904179 66 4 (A limited edition of 150 copies cloth
                          bound, each numbered and signed by the
                          author.)

A catalogue record for this book
is available from the British Library

Cover photograph by Simon Clarke

Printed in Great Britain by Latimer Trend & Company Ltd.,
Plymouth, Devon

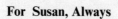

For Susan, Always

Nay: one there is to whom these things,
That nobody else's mind calls back,
Have a savour that scenes in being lack,
And a presence more than the actual brings ...

Thomas Hardy

All these have now a patina of your
body and mind, a kind of ghostly glow
which haloes them a little, though invisible.

Iain Crichton Smith

I thought if I could draw my paines
Through Rimes vexation, I should them allay,
Griefe brought to numbers cannot be so fierce,
For, he tames it, that fetters it in verse.

John Donne

CONTENTS

COCOON

let the world rage

my love moves quietly
as apple-blossom blown
by a small wind or words
unspoken like the touch of her name

let it rage

BURNING OFF PAINT

in an upstairs room
to make a place for my new-born daughter
meant nozzled hissing heat, blistering
layers away, the window wide
for fumes to escape and for air.

At an awkward corner the blue roar
stopped, when the canister leaked
and caught fire. Only one place
for the lot to go—
onto the lawn below.

The instant fire fell
from my hand to the green
I saw the pram with my baby girl
left there to sleep. My mind
flashed leap out, smother the blast,
but the cylinder bounced
a yard from her pram and burst.
She slept on. Sanding the years away
in that room, I stare down,
still feeling the need of that fall.

BY THE SEA

Watching you edge
down the cliff path, slipping
slightly, nervous at each sandy turn
(the baby clasped to your shoulder,
me with the folded push-chair)
till coarse grass gives way to pebbles —
how glad I am to be young
and in your company always.

August. A radiant day. Few
know this beach; no one knows us.
We are secret, special.

Reaching the sand's wet line,
you dabble her toes in the foam,
amused by her gurgles and squeaks.
I stand and gaze at a ship
which slowly divides the horizon.
Between that line and this
time gathers, swells, rolls on,
as our married years will.

Turning, I notice a ringlet of hair,
moist on your sun-flecked brow,
the love of our child in your eyes,
a deepness, the wisdom of motherhood.

THE NEW SECRETARY

I knew she was bright
when I watched her, three,
first answer the telephone.

She waited until its
dangerous ringing
stopped; then picked
the receiver up and said, "Hello."

*

A few years later I happened
to ask, "Do you know why
you see lightning flash
before you hear thunder?"

She paused for a moment;
then said, "Because my eyes
are in front of my ears."

THE HEART

How did her heart
come to be hurt
so much? Was it
because old age
had hit it hard?

Or did his love
languish and die?
The latter, yes.
She was still young.

That, when it went,
left her nothing
to do but age
and slowly edge
into the dark.

GHOSTS

live in our garden. One stands
with a big giraffe, stares at the flash
and has vanished. One lounges against your skirt,
thumb in mouth, looks solemn and fades.
Look! There's another one in blue
with small fast legs, crashing
a tricycle on the ringing gate.
Racing a cat to sandpit
and slide, it disappears.

Other ghosts, too, wander the afternoon.
Wrinkled, not so steady, talking too much
but kind, coming out of the shadows of two world wars
to no greater peace of mind, there they are:
standing outside the gate and looking in.

IDYLL IN EARLY MARCH

Today the sky's grey wall
has a brilliant small
gate, where streaming light
sparkles, as though millions of bright
souls are singing there despite
the cold. All would be well if we knew
and could prove that singing was there. You
and I would at last understand
what seems always hidden from view:
human love with all its imperfections
is worthy of grace and
mirrors those sunlit reflections.

MEDITATIONS IN A PARK

Late summer nights I'd stand
in a cool/warm wind on the field
and gaze at the darkening beech,
vague trees beyond. The land
ended there. But trees never concealed
the moon where the sky began
and the first faint stars grew, each
a question, a message, a plan?

Many years on it's the same:
none of it understood—which is odd,
for science has vastly improved
knowledge of moon and stars. Though the name
we give to their maker is God,
confronted by all that wonder I'm still
not sure the little word *love*
applies, but I trust it will.

ON A WINTRY SHORE

The sea collapses to lace and pushes a purled
irregular line where we stand, looking across the bay.
Further out strong waves collide
with an armoury of rocks and explode. The spray,
flung high and wide, subsides in the next blue-
green gathering swell, ceaselessly gripped and hurled
by millions of centuries of moon to
moan and slide.

But here, though blown and cold, we're safe to watch
storm-water and clouds, the last wolf or bear
long gone and no vile reptile stalking our lives;
safe but reminded, again, by the wind's tear-
ing shriek of our own kind's screams, which lunge
out of Russia or somewhere, and we catch
sight of creatures that hack and plunge
through the struggling air like gulls or knives.

HIS BABY GIRL

Her life lasted only
a day; perfect, till
one heart-stopping
moment left him
in shock and with tears
seeking reasons or words.

None could be found. He goes
each year to her grave
in the north, takes
a few flowers,
reflects on past lives
for some consolation.

None can be found. Only
her name on a stone
stands up to time.
Rain and chill winds
whip leaves where he walks,
encountering shadows.

TO A BLACKBIRD

You've been at it all afternoon,
ripping out moss among
the pond's marsh marigolds. You hop
on rocks, then fly back,
but knowing the neighbourhood
don't go straight home. You take steps:
the fence, the cherry tree, are stops
to deceive cats, magpies, me, until
you vanish into Barbara's conifer.

Your beak's green fronds will soften
the earlier wickerwork. Skilled
in upholstery, did
you and your mate agree
on the carpet's colour, on matching cushions?
Such a plush lining
of intricate wispy twigs may be
a sign of instinctive good taste,
but I think much more is built
into your house and mine: that warmth
which sustains our fragile clinging-on.

SARAH, TRAVELLING

Driving from Belle Vue home, I saw—
was it?—that girl I passed in a flash—
my daughter, her hair dropping over her face,
a heavy bag slung over her bowed shoulder?

I braked, but missed the turn and then went on.
Six years too late. No going back
to embarrass a stranger or find again
heroin's persistent point in Sarah's eyes.

In late October sunshine
students, walking to restaurants or pubs
or a park with friends, were talking
of love, no doubt, and politics
and beer and what our purpose is
in being here. Each fair, vivacious girl recalled
my daughter heading for the hostel's homeless rooms.

Unsettled, yes, those last few miles.
Then I reached home. And there
instead of family and friends we share
abandoned things: books, pictures, tapes,
a teddy bear. This empty car.

AT CONISTON

The trees burned yellow and brown, green,
golden and red down the road from Skelwith Bridge.
At Yew Tree Tarn we stopped
to watch the reeds and the light on the water.

Now, on this high terrace,
gently surprised we catch in the evening air
coal fumes from the houses below,
where friendly lights shine.

The mountains deepen. The forest
darkens and the town. As dark
seeps into the lake, bright stars
appear to sail across the sky,

as if to suggest we too must shape ourselves
for a journey. Ah, there's no shelter,
my love, from the night, though we return
to the cottage door and go in.

EPITHALAMIUM ON LUCY'S DAY

The song's out of fashion in these days
of obscene magazines and videos—
romance, an old sock, flung away.
On Lucy's wedding day no
shepherds pipe, no zephyrs blow
lily and primrose. No woodland sprites are dancing
to a satyr's tambourine. Pan doesn't sing.

Still, this is Lucy's day. Intermittent rain
soaks the bowling-green in Hale
and shoppers, parking cars on the main
road, observe their own solemnities and trail
in search of Safeway trolleys. She can't fail
to make each wedding guest adore her warm
smile and graceful form.

Since Pan is absent, all I can offer
is an ordinary prayer
that in this marriage her
love will be magical, rare
as a unicorn, and no demon dwell there.
Let her like mistletoe
cherish the oak where love grows.

With reverence may
her bridegroom bring her bliss-
ful gently home and say,
"So let us rest, sweet love, in hope of this."

LANCASTRIA

in memory of Sydney Clarke (1915–1940)
and his comrades

When he grew up, his parents knew
their youngest son was born for war.
They saw the second coming.
He thought only of the girl
he'd one day marry. "I'll wait for you,"
she said, giving him so much hope.

But other things excited him
one cloudless, summer afternoon
which turned to uproar as the planes flew in
and set about their work. His ship
was bombed, bombed, bombed, belched fire,
sank in twenty minutes into burning oil.
At least five thousand men were killed.

I try to imagine the terror
he felt, if (not lucky enough to be
dead in an instant explosion of blood)
he found himself, lacking eyes or a leg,
waltzed to death by the insane water
or trapped in seething iron and steam,
knowing he'd never get out, his scream
turning to bubbles in the grey Atlantic...

Then the waiting, several years, for news.

The "Lancastria" was sunk by the Luftwaffe on 17th June, 1940
off the coast of St. Nazaire. Winston Churchill decided the news
had to be kept secret, because the disaster came so soon after Dunkirk,
but it was an embargo he forgot to lift.

VISITING GRANDMA

On Tuesday nights in Winter our star-ship
raced to the past. In Summer
we walked the long roads. Men who attacked
from mountainous gardens I killed.

I recall the grim hallway,
its monstrous plant in a pot,
the kettle's rattle on the room's black range
and the backyard privy, where squares
of newspaper hung on a string.

I steered my solid lead battleship
over an armchair of seas and spoke
only when spoken to. Grandma told
my mother the same tales week after week.
Torpedoed, I fired the rescue flares.
Abandon ship! Abandon ship!

She was harmless and kind, I suppose,
but came from a horse-drawn world and lived
in a joyless house with gas lamps, unlit.
In her crinkled, black, Victorian dress
she'd stoop to rake the fire, brew tea
and bring dry biscuits or cake.

She was too old to love.
Adrift on a swelling sea, I wondered
what I, a commander of ships at eight,
was doing there and on what dismal shore
my small life-raft would one day land.

MEETING PLACES

I saw him, once:
a shadow, silent
at a velvet-covered table;
I, four or five; he, faceless
with a mug of tea
in that dark room.

No voice or gesture; just
bowed shadow, dead in 1944
before I learned to count the days.

Last week at a whim
I went in search of his origins
and waited, in another room, for an event
to become a document,
for a name on a grave to be born.

A red certificate: my grandfather
(numbered in 1877) named
by William and Mary (formerly Park)
hiding behind their names.
But column 7 carries the shock:
"X the mark of Mary Clark, mother,
25 Dearden Street, Hulme."

That cross, more eloquent than a kiss,
lays her bare. What can be said,
except there's a likelihood the sun,
getting her out of bed, set fire
to whatever girlish dreams she may have had
and put her to drudge at a scrubbing-board,
which taught her to limit her own horizons?

AN AFFIRMATION

If I could snatch
light in my hand like thistle-down
floating to autumn soil, or catch
time tuning the red-berried air
and hold the note, the moment there,
would I be nearer knowing
what lit the dragonfly and is sowing
age in my face and hands?

Catch light? I cannot, nor know
into what darkness I must go.
Does every sojourner at prayer
kneeling alone
below sacred names
where sunlight illuminates the dust on stone
find only quietness remains,
that words are absorbed by air?

We are made to live here
with things that existed before they had names
against the days of meteoric rock and ice-age.
Above, the nuclear heavens rage.
What fashioned them
has fashioned us, a stratagem
which leaves us little choice but to make
something for our own sakes—
love: the mysterious best expression
of what we are
on this small planet, whose progression
seems otherwise arbitrary among indifferent stars.

JOURNEYING

Surely it won't be down there?
Turn left at the inn and first right
he said, but here are only small
sad caravans and a store which is closed.

On down a deep lane: the nettled banks
brushing the car; grass, dandelions
crowning the broken road, nothing
coming the other way. And then

the soundless opening to heat
and stunning isolation of white sands.
We face the sun across an empty sea:
a lovely genesis, keeping its secret still.

WALKING WITH HER

We both love the evening peace,
that line of poplars, the elm,
this sweep of lawn, but none of it
cares for us. Our pleasure is
the price we pay for being here,
our rent.

                All these paths
lead to loss, my love, and when
one of us goes, the other
will only know the wind will
settle for desolation,
unlike the stadium's roar before
it reaches the evening news
in a humped, dark town.

THE WILLOW

Great willow
filling from far my window
I lie in my bedroom and see
you fur with green.
I have seen you stark
for long months, lifting
a huge V
from the dark
world of tubers and clay
to the thin snows.
I saw you let go
your leaves, as if they
had never been,
and stand
in a dead land
with frost drifting.

You looked dead,
but now sew
sleeves with green thread.
Perhaps when my slow
stitching to marl by worm
is done, from my rooted cell
I could confirm
my spirit lives
fresh in another fashion
to one who lies
troubled, where I once lay.
The sign you give
I'd give. Her intuition
would hear me tell
green-tongued tales from clay
and see love light my greening eyes.

MATTERS OF COURSE

> "...& poor Mrs. Wright what a breach Death makes in our
> acquaintance every time he pays a visit among them & what
> an imperceptible impression such visits make with the world.
> The newspapers are read by thousands & the Thousands of
> deaths in them are passed over as matters of course but the
> loss is only felt by the few..."
>
> John Clare: *Letter to John Taylor*,
> 15 November, 1829

Watching bombs or rebellious cells on TV,
viewers can comment safely on things going wrong.
Remote, they feel in control. It's more disconcerting to be
there at a woman's collapse, when she smashes the floor, scattering
the supermarket trolleys. Death turns chattering
customers away, is cordoned off, played down. And the day
carries on with the manager's apologies, pools news, birdsong,
but on this occasion there's no slow-motion replay.

And in the large, famous, imposing hospitals where fate
is properly catered for, lingers the odd refusal
by visitors scanning old magazines to contemplate
facts: that a loved one is coming to the end of choice,
that by degrees in deeper rooms off corridors a voice
hoarse, breathless, will be heard for the last
time. This has nothing to do with the perusal
of newspapers or sunshine and cannot be bypassed.

Even so, tall buses run past the hospital gates
every hour and take numbed relatives home through the sprawl
of shops and cinemas, offices, houses, parks, to the far-flung estates
where they'll sit with the *Get Well* cards. Later a priest may call.

DAFFODILS

I wanted to keep
if I could,
a curl
at the nape of her neck
lovingly for ever,
light as a summer breeze
or blown as snowdrops are blown,

for its scent was sweetly sown
with most precious heart's-ease,
but death came to sever
its silken ring and wreck
the girl
who once stood
where daffodils leap.

ELEGY
for my wife

1

She died on the last day
of the last year, when snow
came falling out of the fairy tale
and there was nowhere else to go.

These are the darkest
of all days
ever I have known.

Always I awaken
to the one thought:
Susan has died.

2

A still day.
Winter light
sweeps the lawn and hedges
and my slow fingers
seek to hold what lingers
of her spirit in the hushed house
and things she made bright:
her bed, bookcase, that green-
striped chair, a pen, these clothes.

Time has slowed, too:
rooms with her laughter
stilled, filled
with unanswerable silence,
an altered state of being.
I look through dulled
windows on a world
which daily passes by,
the garden gripped in frost,
the sun gone down.

And I am stilled, transmuted
into something I have never
been. "David,
I'm strange!" she cried
through her drugged suffering
three days before she died.

I am her residue of pain.

3

Rain has set in,
blurring the street's amber lamps.
I wonder what it is like
to have no earthly form,
to be transformed.

Say, rather, she
has taken fear
of death away
and in her going
left a longing.

4

Now she lies
with cornstalk and leaf
and I walk
unending avenues of grief.

Some say she is in God's care
and I cannot believe
such goodness as hers
does not still exist somewhere.

5

She did not die in this house,
but in a careful room
not far from here. I was there
when she went patiently away,
drifting like the perfume from a gift
of hyacinths, as snowflakes fell
past the window pane. She went home.

My kiss gave her release,
as if she waited
for a sign,
then sank to peace.

Now, unseen, I hope she is everywhere—
her hazel eyes, her elegant hands
and honey-coloured hair—
in this bedroom, on the attic stair,
crossing the lawn to stand
and gaze at the pond and the life there.

But she is utterly changed.
Does she now roam the orchard land
this house was built on
in an age of carriages and steam?
Does she know villein and reeve, Roman,
the primal forest and rock?

Her time is no longer mine,
but if I could see her again,
lifting her arms to love me again
or turning her face to be kissed,
I'd be content. If I could
hear her voice again — but she
is utterly different now:
different, silent, timeless as the light
that flickers through the willow's leaves
and makes them shine like tears.

NOW AND THEN

Strolling in the garden after rain,
our cat sniffing the box hedge by the gate,
see! the first newts of Spring,
the pond's annual courtship. Everything
fresh: the lawn's scent, the silver birch
dripping, purple primulas, daffodils,
spawn. Always like this?

Inside, I leaf through the photographs
you labelled so carefully before your death:
schoolfriends, relatives, dates, names, places.

Now and what was: an old house,
the Lakes, the Oxford Summer Ball,
weekend visits to Plas Teg Hall—
all saying then, then, then.
Frozen moments never to come again.

IN A GARDEN

Woman much missed, I will never say
our love's at an end, though you left on a lengthening day
and live now in my turbulent mind,
where I travel to find you
(equable, young, and kind
as you were and remain) who

had the most generous heart of any
one I have ever known. Many
a time, watching the birch tree's slow
yellowing, where we walked late in love,
I pray you are safe and approve
my search for providence in the fall of a sparrow.

Who am I to say whether your new
world, if it exists, makes you
happier, even in bliss? Such talk
troubles grief. Was your departing
indeed like this flower stalk
that rots in the ground to rise next Spring?

FUGITIVES

"Rapt, twirling in thy hand a wither'd spray,
And waiting for the spark from heaven to fall."

The Scholar-Gipsy, Matthew Arnold

From a pear-tree's shade, where the lawn
drifts to spent lilac and laburnum, I hear hot broom
crack and water fall to the pond and, beyond,
the motorway's dim humming. Home
on the rim of this north-west centre of trade
and industry and hooting trams is the place,
if anywhere, to recover hope or at least
some sense of the ideal the Scholar-Gipsy has—
who we must imagine exempt from age
and rarely seen round here: wandering once
by the river Dane; in dappled
Delamere one summer evening, or
battling against the snow on the moor
above Macclesfield, striding towards
a hill where the true light might finally
break out far more spectacularly
than that other bright fugitive of ice and gas
crossing the constellations, its incandescent
head and tail sewn into chronicles, equally
at home in the future as in the past.

SORROW AND HOPE

Dear ghost I sense in the April air,
fine, like a song ending, but still there,
you are not like the ghosts who may stray
through the altered garden, who lived
in these different rooms before we were born,
their acts and love they called home forgotten
except by the brickwork, past recall
all but our own homemaking under these eaves.

No, I know you too well. We have
too much in common still. You have not
gone to ground, where your ashes lie
this third April turning to May
since that raw winter day
of shocked, hopeful scattering.

But I should have known love
leads to parting, can't reconcile
death with the living. There has
to be more than drink, tears, despair.

Dear ghost, I try to believe
your laughter, courage and kindness
continue in other forms, that you
are always in every place
and I will merge with your mystery
some day. Let it be so.

CHETTLE HOUSE

The pamphlet's photographs show a stylish house
the other side of cared-for lawns and gardens
against a blue sky. It tells Chettle's
story from ancient settlements to when

the house was built in the eighteenth century.
The rounded corners are impressive; so, too,
a central staircase and drawing-room.
The word that springs to mind is *civilised*.

Of course, the house had periods of neglect
and alteration, but its restoration
struck two visitors, a man and wife,
who later let the pamphlet gather dust

with some other guide books on an attic shelf
ten years or more. Found again, it's comforting
to think those two once called at this house,
lived in and loved, and as deep as England.

They shared a sense of time's silence at the house
that Summer, but into that silence his wife
has gone, and most of his own life now
like that splendid Summer is out of reach.

IN NORBURY CHURCH

The years go by, years
spent in growing old
to no purpose, except to find
that getting over your death
is a kind of disloyalty
nothing will alter.

Thirty-five years ago
we married here. I stand
where we stood, Susan, thinking
now of our shared past,
while a workman whistles
and a strong wind stirs the grass
around your parents' grave.

Yes, I am me still, trapped
in these later years, you
belonging to the gracious dead,
you who loved people, loved to please,
with never a trace of self-regard.

"I don't mind dying, if I didn't feel
so ill," you said. In those last months
I think you sensed some transcendental thing
we didn't talk about...both of us lost for words?

ABSENCES

This is another Spring
you haven't seen,
since the willow
went down, our herald
of the year's awakening.

For three days
I heard his saw, watched
the man, helmeted
like a ladybird,
stick to his task
and cut down our glory,
cylinders of dead wood
thumping the ground.

Like you the willow has died.
It once filled the sky.
Now there is only
vast, blue, empty
evidence of change.

MARRIED LOVE
for Simon and Karen

May you
always rejoice in your hearts
that the other was born.

And may
each of you carefully guard
the other's solitude.

31st DECEMBER
1898, 1996

Summer has long gone, its days
drained to darkness, the sun
not seen, or low, a light
behind trees. My mother was born
on this day, the day my wife died
several family lifetimes later.
Ninety-eight years: more than enough
to point out mortality
in letters and photographs.

In a few weeks the gardener will come
to tend the lawns round the church.
Making use of a rising light
to inspect the raked moss,
he'll be mostly concerned
with plantains, sweeping, clearing away
and may not notice the steeple
pointing to something else:
something like love, or a new start.

TO MY GRANDSON
William Rowland Clarke

Small, helpless, three days old,
you need cuddles and milk
to keep you from the cold,
your warm cocoon exchanged
for giant shadows, voices, hands
with things to do for your benefit.
You bring many congratulations
but as yet have no idea
how to smile. You suck, yell, sleep.

How will you fare? All wish you well:
health, strength, happiness, a fine mind
to go with good looks—plenty
of fortune-telling, in other words,
on colourful greetings-cards.
I'll not add to the list.

Instead, I issue a warning note—
time continues to tick, young man,
whatever you hit upon as you grow
through the wonderful, troubled years—
and advice which is equally plain
and equally hard to fulfil:
be kind, treasure friends, love life every day.

MAX

"You can't get angry with him,"
his mother said, "or impose
your rules. There are no rules.
His life is not like that."

I watch Max crawl, head down,
his fair hair flopping, through the tall
conversation and trousered pine-trees
of the sitting-room. The talk is about
a baby who's been baptised
this afternoon and who waves
and smiles, as babies do.

Not like Max. It's easy to say
what he can't do at four: walk,
talk, eat without a stomach tube,
or look at you straight. "He can cling on
when he wants your attention," she said.

Max reaches the coloured lights of a toy
he dimly sees and loves. He seems
content to be not of our world
but in it. "And it's no use
wanting the child you didn't have,"
his mother says, hoisting him up.

There are no rules, but Max
has influence and helps his mother
turn the challenge of her life to love.

Beneath this white moon
grotesque, autumnal shadows
dance against the wall.

Snowflakes lovingly
touched her gold hair like a crown.
Do you remember?

At the end of life,
a petal shed on water,
ripples glint and smile.

The river runs deep,
but no deeper than its spring
or my love for her.

Apple-blossom curls
in a wind which eddies round
the ancient gardens.